Ralph Baer

The Man Behind Video Games

Nancy Dickmann

raintree

a Capstone company — publishers for children

Raintree is an imprint of Capstone Global Library Limited, a company incorporated in England and Wales having its registered office at 264 Banbury Road, Oxford, OX2 7DY – Registered company number: 6695582

www.raintree.co.uk
myorders@raintree.co.uk

Editor: Jill Kalz
Designer: Kayla Rossow
Media researcher: Svetlana Zhurkin
Original illustrations © Capstone Global Library Limited 2020
Production Specialist: Tori Abraham
Originated by Capstone Global Library Ltd
Printed and bound in India

ISBN 978 1 4747 8678 2 (hardback)
ISBN 978 1 4747 8686 7 (paperback)

British Library Cataloguing in Publication Data
A full catalogue record for this book is available from the British Library.

Acknowledgements
We would like to thank the following for permission to use photographs: Alamy: Chris Willson, 24, Interfoto, 22, John Henshall, 10; AP Photo: cover (back), 5, Pablo Martinez Monsivais, 26; National Archives and Records Administration, 11; Newscom: akg-images, 14, picture-alliance/dpa/Jens Wolf, 21, 29; Shutterstock: Andrey Popov, 4, Everett Historical, 7, 9, 12, James Steidl, 15, Sergey Novikov, 17, Monkey Business Images, 28; Smithsonian Institution: National Museum of American History, 6, 8, 27, National Museum of American History/Ralph H. Baer, cover (inset), 16, 18, 19, 20, 25; Wikimedia: Evan-Amos, 23, U.S. Navy, 13. Design Elements by Shutterstock.

Our thanks to Emma Grahn, Spark!Lab Manager, Lemelson Center for the Study of Invention and Innovation, National Museum of American History, USA, for her invaluable help in the preparation of this book. We would also like to thank Kealy Gordon, Product Development Manager, and the following at Smithsonian Enterprises: Ellen Nanney, Licensing Manager; Brigid Ferraro, Vice President, Education and Consumer Products; and Carol LeBlanc, Senior Vice President, Education and Consumer Products.

3800 19 0053664 4

HIGH LIFE HIGHLAND

CONTENTS

INTRODUCTION

Do you play video games? You might play them on a computer. Maybe you use a smartphone or a tablet. Some types of video games link up to your TV. This is how the earliest home video games worked. They were invented by a man named Ralph Baer.

People play video games all around the world.

Ralph Baer is known as the "father of the home video game".

Baer was an inventor. Inventors come up with new ideas for things. Then they build them. They test and tweak them until they have a product that works. Inventions shape our everyday lives.

MOVING TO AMERICA

Ralph Baer was born in Germany in 1922. Baer and his family were Jewish. When Baer was 11 years old he had to leave school. The German government, led by Adolf Hitler, decided that Jewish children should not be allowed to go to school.

The Baers had family members in the United States. Their family members helped the Baers escape from Germany in 1938. They sailed to the United States to live.

Baer was 1 year old when this photo was taken.

Adolf Hitler and the Nazi Party controlled Germany for 12 years.

NAZI GERMANY

In 1933 Adolf Hitler became the leader of Germany. He was part of a group called the Nazis. The Nazis wanted someone to blame for Germany's poverty after World War I (1914–18). They wrongly blamed the Jewish people and murdered millions of them.

STARTING WORK

New York became the Baers' new home. Baer was 16 years old and he got a job in a factory. In his free time, Baer studied radios. He learned to build and fix them. He set up a business. But then, in 1939, World War II started. Baer joined the US Army. He was now a US citizen.

Baer served in the US Army.

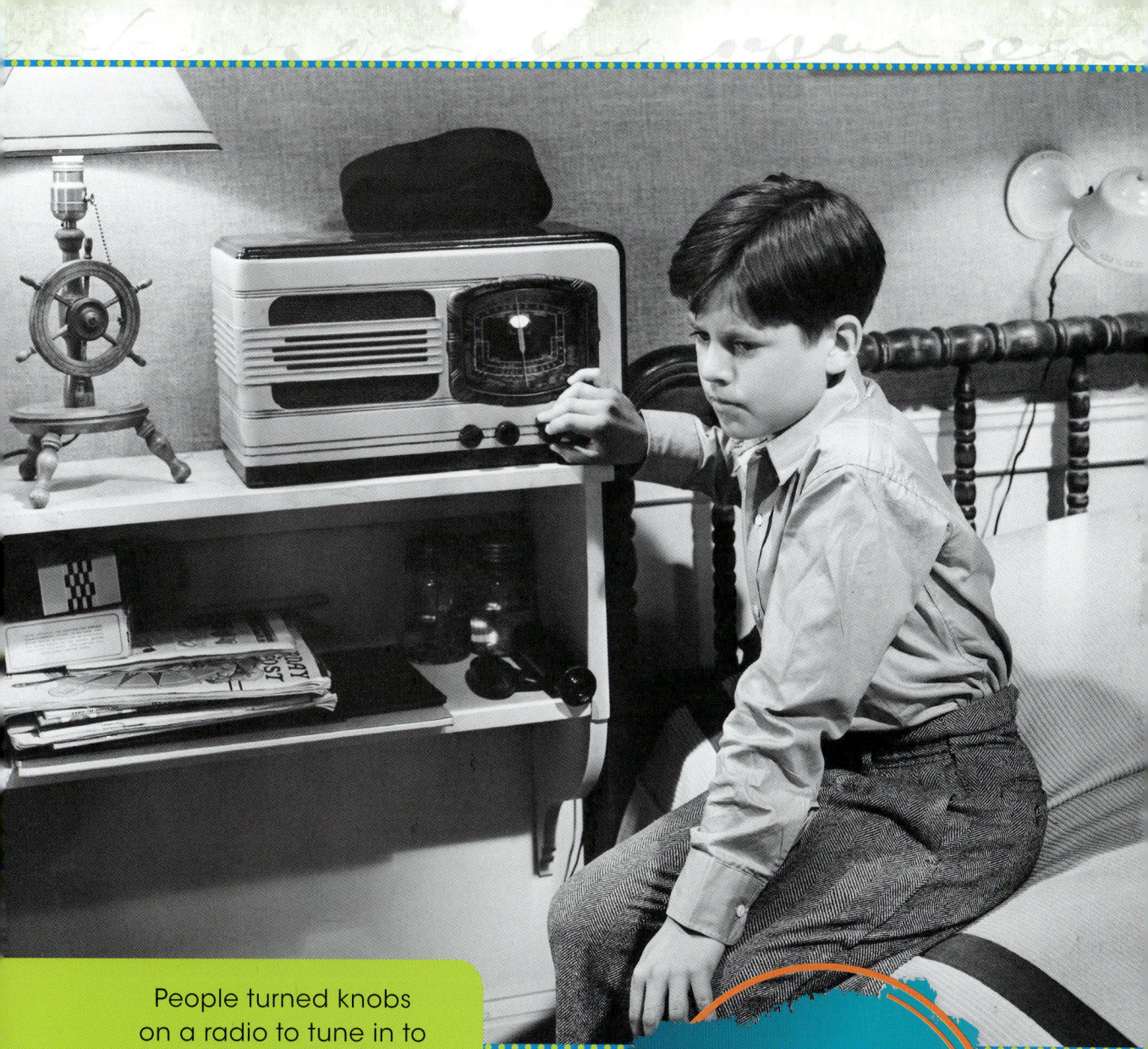

People turned knobs on a radio to tune in to different stations.

In the 1930s most people had radios. They listened to music, plays and news reports.

ENGINEERING

When World War II ended, Baer returned home. He didn't go back to fixing radios. He decided to go to university instead. He wanted to learn how TVs worked.

This is what the inside of a 1948 TV looked like.

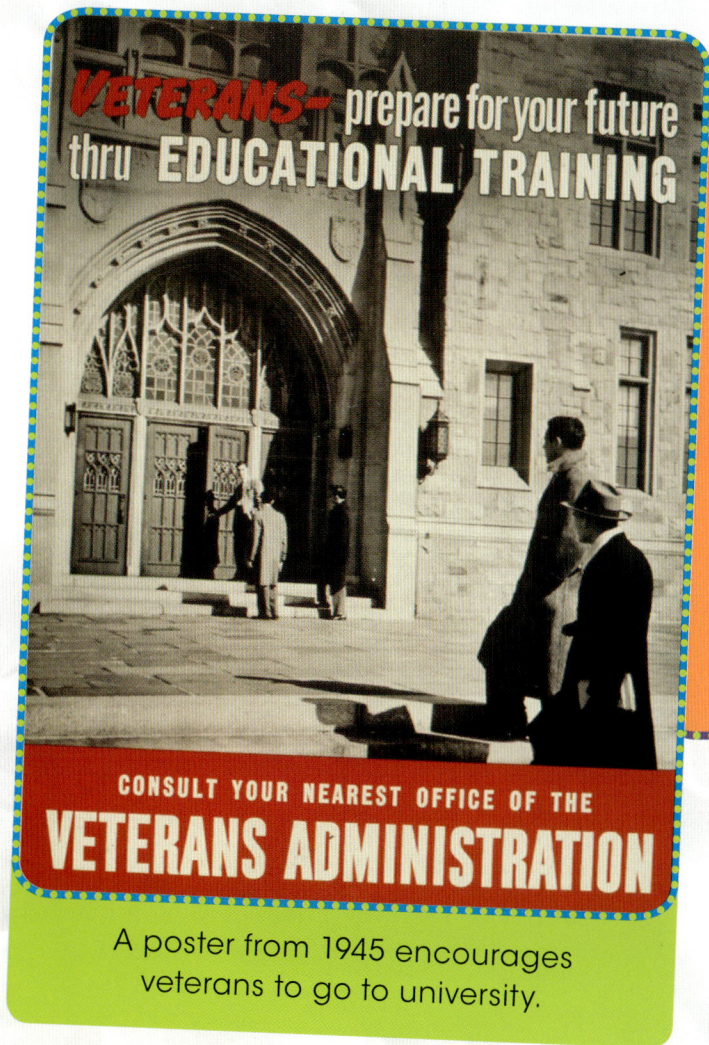

VETERANS– prepare for your future thru EDUCATIONAL TRAINING

CONSULT YOUR NEAREST OFFICE OF THE
VETERANS ADMINISTRATION

A poster from 1945 encourages veterans to go to university.

THE GI BILL

The GI Bill was a law to help soldiers like Baer. It was passed at the end of the war. Ex-soldiers, known as "veterans", could get a loan to buy a home. They could go to university for free.

Baer went to university in Chicago. He trained as a TV engineer. Engineers use science to make or improve products. Baer moved back to New York. He started his new career as an engineer.

MOVING UP

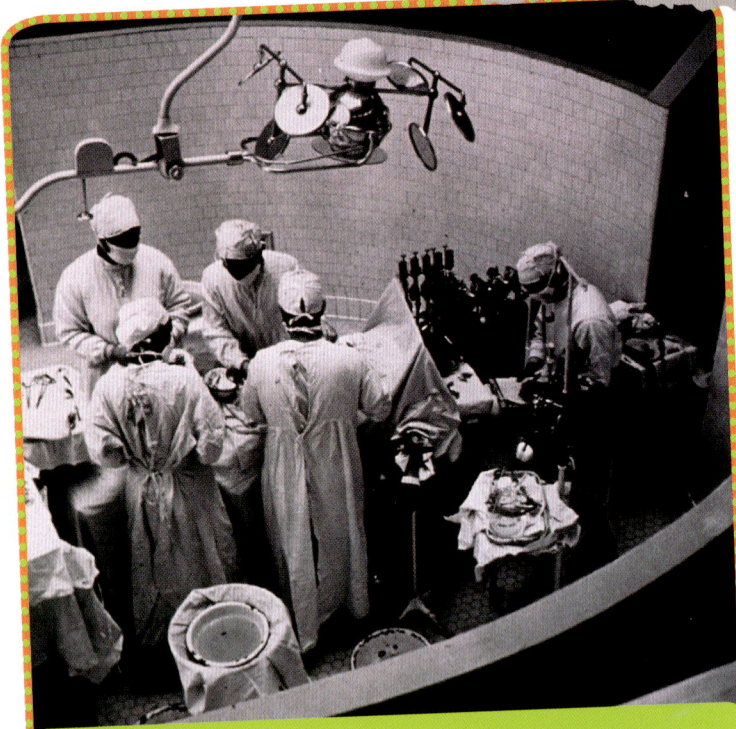

In the 1950s, Baer and other engineers designed new tools for medical operations.

Baer had learned about electronics. These skills helped him get a job. But it was not with TVs. Instead he designed medical tools. Baer was good at his job. He kept moving on to better work.

Baer joined a company called Sanders Associates. He was in charge of 500 engineers. Sanders sold electronics to the US Army. They made systems for planes. They also made equipment for NASA.

NASA stands for National Aeronautics and Space Administration. The US government started NASA in 1958.

Baer and other Sanders engineers built electronic systems for military planes.

THE RISE OF TELEVISION

In 1950, TV was new. Only a small number of homes had one. There were not many channels. But more and more people bought TVs. They were excited by this new technology.

There were news and comedy shows on TV. But all you could do was watch. One day Baer had an idea. What if you could play games on your TV?

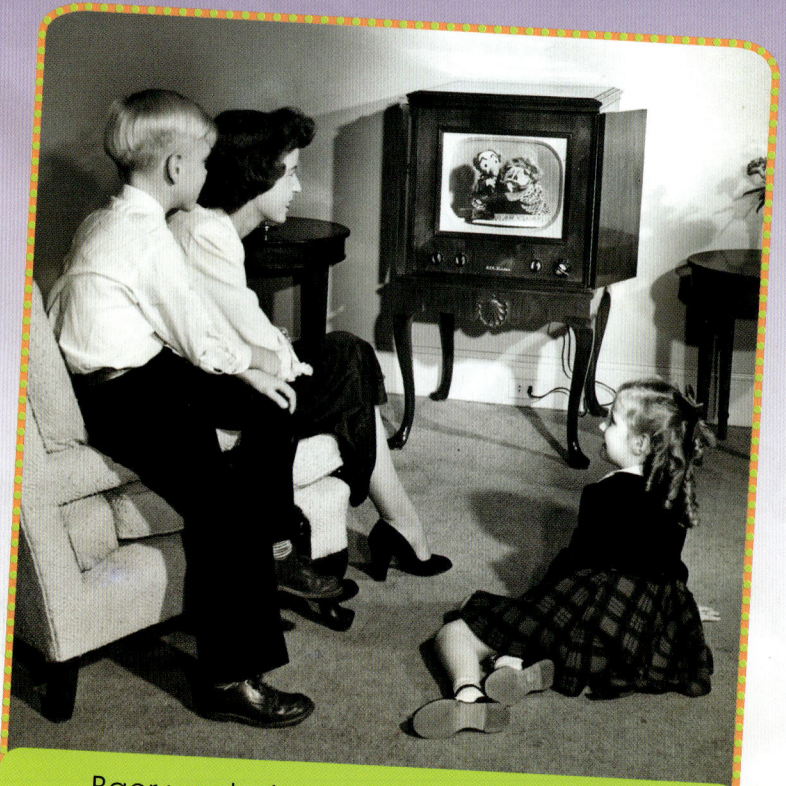

Baer wanted people to communicate with a TV, not just watch it.

PERCENTAGE OF HOMES IN THE UNITED STATES WITH A TV (1950-1960)

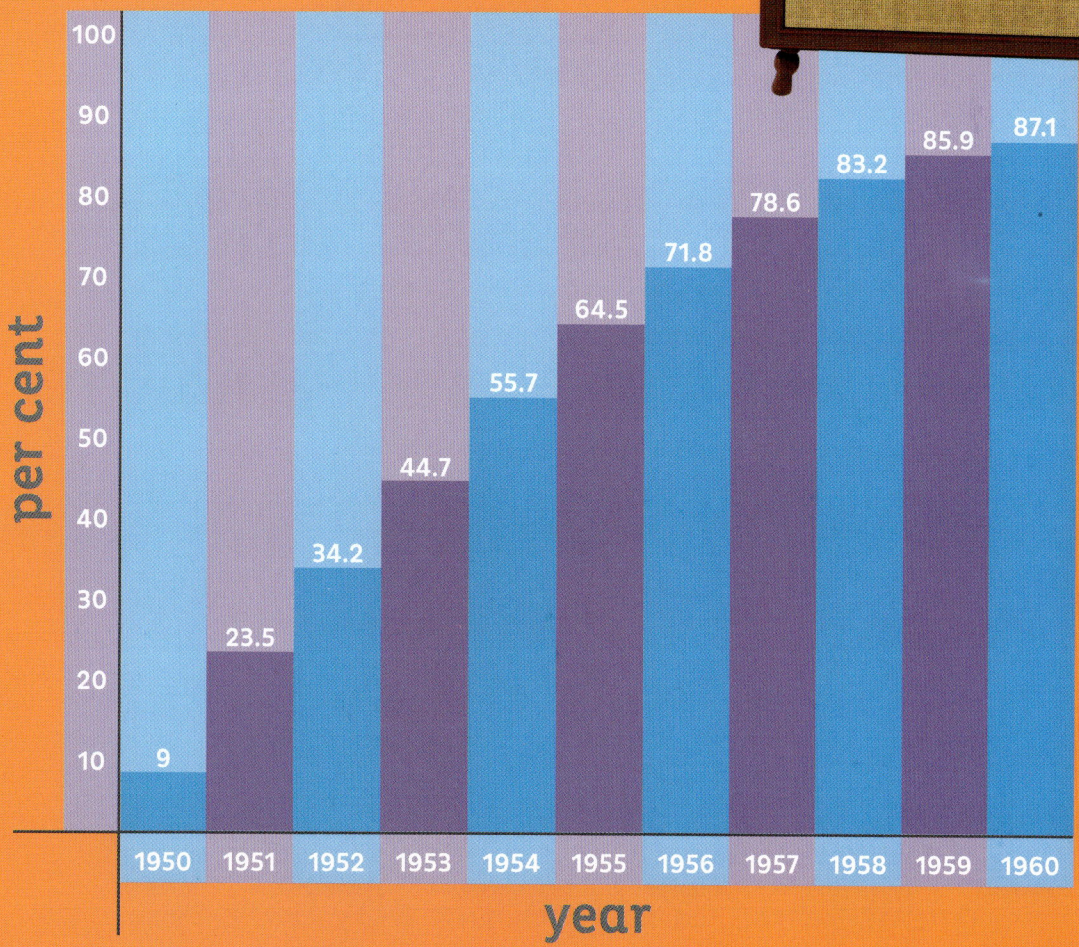

Bar chart showing per cent on the vertical axis (0 to 100) and year on the horizontal axis (1950–1960):

Year	Per cent
1950	9
1951	23.5
1952	34.2
1953	44.7
1954	55.7
1955	64.5
1956	71.8
1957	78.6
1958	83.2
1959	85.9
1960	87.1

WORK BEGINS

Baer made this sketch of his idea on 6 September 1966.

Baer sketched out his ideas. He thought about how a games console might work. Could people play hockey or football on a TV? What about draughts, ping-pong or card games?

By the 1960s, most homes had TVs. Baer thought many people might buy a games console. Baer's boss wasn't sure at first. But he let Baer try out his idea. He assigned two engineers to help Baer. They were Bill Harrison and Bill Rusch.

Ping-pong was one of the games Baer wanted people to play with a games console.

MAKING A PROTOTYPE

Inventors make prototypes to see if their ideas work. Then they tweak them and try again. Baer's team found a way to make a moving dot on a TV screen. Next they made a way to control it. A player could move the dot around.

They made a box with chase games and shooting games. Baer kept improving it. In 1967, he finished his seventh version. It had two controllers. It could play many games. Baer called it the "Brown Box".

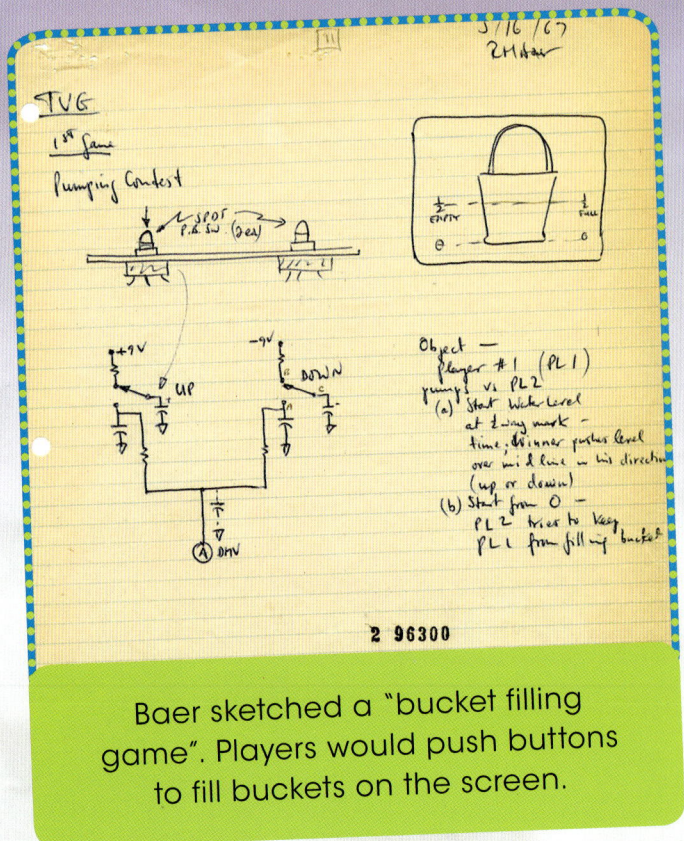

Baer sketched a "bucket filling game". Players would push buttons to fill buckets on the screen.

The Brown Box was first known as TV Game Unit no.7.

Players flipped switches on the front of the Brown Box to play games. The index cards were the programs for the games, such as ping-pong, draughts and golf putting.

INNOVATING

A light gun was used to play a target practice game on the Brown Box.

The light gun and four target games were later sold separately from the games console.

Baer had a lot of ideas. He wanted to make the games even more fun. He bought a cheap plastic toy gun. He put a sensor inside it. It could sense light from the TV screen.

The light gun could "shoot" at the screen. Players could hit a target. Baer's bosses liked the Brown Box. It was time to sell Baer's invention.

Baer and his team covered the Brown Box with sticky vinyl that looked like wood.

SUCCESS!

Sanders sold the idea to Magnavox.
Magnavox was a company that made TVs.
They turned Baer's
prototype into a
slick product.
They called it the
"Magnavox Odyssey".

FACTS ABOUT THE ODYSSEY

Release date
September 1972

Price
about £80

Games
12

Power source
Six C batteries

Controllers
2

Number sold
350,000

The Odyssey came with sheets of coloured plastic. They stuck to the TV screen. They made the games look more exciting.

Two players could play the games. There was no colour or sound. But there was nothing else like it! People loved it. Other companies started to make their own games consoles.

OTHER GAMES

Baer was hooked! He wanted to keep making electronic games. One of his new designs was called "Simon". It was based on Simon Says.

Each button on Simon plays a different note. The sounds are based on the four notes a bugle makes.

Simon was popular with families.

Up to four people could play Maniac at one time.

"Coming up with [new] ideas and converting them into real products has always been as natural as breathing for me."

—Ralph Baer

To play Simon, you had to copy the notes it played. It was released in 1978. The game was a huge hit. Baer made a similar game, "Maniac" in 1979. Maniac was harder to play. It was not as popular.

LATER LIFE

George W. Bush awarding Baer with the National Medal of Technology

People gave Baer awards for his work. In 2006, the US President at the time, George W. Bush, gave him a medal. It is called the National Medal of Technology. In 2010 Baer's name was added to the National Inventors Hall of Fame.

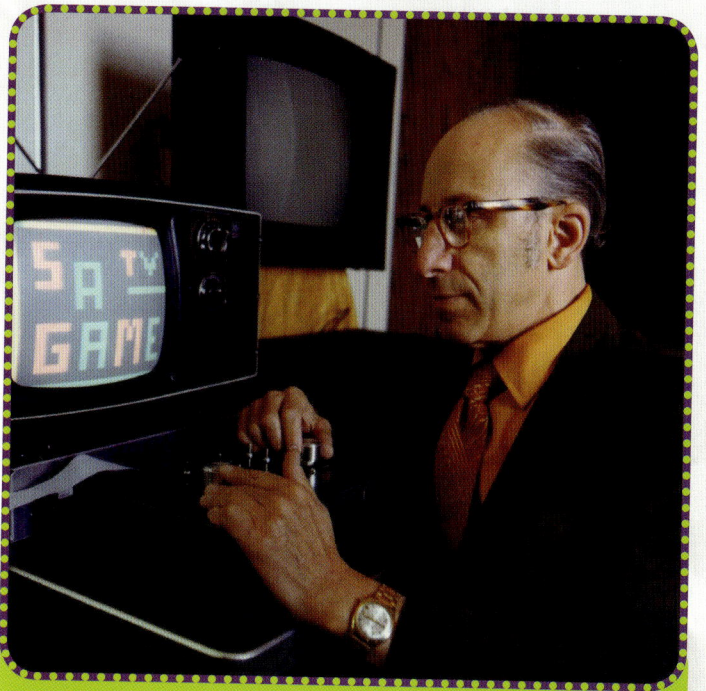

Baer demonstrated his Telesketch game in 1977.

Baer's real workshop is on display at the Smithsonian's National Museum of American History in Washington DC.

"I need a challenge . . . I still get a big charge out of making something work."

—Ralph Baer

Baer retired, but he kept inventing. He loved it too much to stop. He also gave interviews and wrote books. Baer was 92 when he died in 2014. He had never stopped inventing.

FATHER OF THE HOME VIDEO GAME

The Odyssey was the start of something big. Other companies began making video games. New technology helped. Powerful computer chips were designed. Soon games could be faster, brighter and more complex.

Today virtual reality headsets take video games to new levels.

Baer with the Brown Box in 2009

Today the Sony PlayStation is the most popular video games console. More than 500 million of them have been sold since 1994.

Now we play video games all the time. They let us play sports, make music and hunt for treasure. They open up amazing new worlds. And it all started with Ralph Baer's Brown Box!

GLOSSARY

citizen person who legally belongs to and has the rights and protections of a country

complex complicated; something that has many connected parts

electronics science of electricity and how it is used in various devices

engineer someone trained to design and build machines, vehicles, bridges, roads or other structures

games console electronic device that outputs a signal to display a video game

Nazi member of the National Socialist German Workers' Party led by Adolf Hitler; the Nazis ruled Germany from 1933 to 1945

prototype early model of a new invention made in order to test it out

sensor device that detects changes, such as heat, light, sound or motion

technology machinery and equipment that are made by using scientific knowledge

veteran person who served in the armed forces

COMPREHENSION QUESTIONS

1. Look at the photo on page 14. How are today's TVs the same? How are they different?

2. Pages 9, 14 and 15 discuss home entertainment in the time when Baer was young. How is this different from today's home entertainment?

3. How did Baer's light gun work?

FIND OUT MORE

The Nostalgia Nerd's Retro Tech: Computer, Consoles & Games (Tech Classics), Peter Leigh (Ilex Press, 2018)

Video Game Trivia: What You Never Knew About Popular Games, Design Secrets and the Coolest Characters, Sean McCollum (Raintree, 2018)

Who Invented Home Video Games? Ralph Baer, Mary Kay Carson (Enslow, 2012)

WEBSITES

A biography of Ralph Baer and his inventions
americanhistory.si.edu/collections/object-groups/the-father-of-the-video-game-the-ralph-baer-prototypes-and-electronic-games/biography

Fun facts about Ralph Baer
www.kidzworld.com/article/29808-who-invented-video-games

INDEX